Original title:
Believe in Yourself

Copyright © 2024 Swan Charm Publishing
All rights reserved.

Editor: Jessica Elisabeth Luik
Author: Kätriin Kaldaru
ISBN HARDBACK: 978-9916-86-186-8
ISBN PAPERBACK: 978-9916-86-187-5

Fountain of Trust

In gardens green with secrets kept,
A fountain flows where dreams are met,
The water whispers tales of old,
Where trust, like gold, does unfold.

The bonds we weave in silent night,
Illuminate in morning's light,
As rivers merge, as fates do twine,
Trust becomes our grand design.

Through storms we stand, both strong and true,
Our hearts, a compass guiding through,
The doubts that linger in the air,
Are vanquished by the love we share.

In every droplet, worlds unite,
Reflecting hopes that burn so bright,
A fountain flows, forever just,
A testament to endless trust.

Enduring Spirit

In shadows cast by ancient trees,
Whispers ride the gentle breeze,
A spirit stands with steadfast grace,
Unyielding through time's vast embrace.

Mountains rise and rivers wane,
Yet through all, does hope remain,
An ember in the darkest night,
A beacon yielding purest light.

With every challenge, every test,
Our spirit finds its place to rest,
In hearts that beat with fervent dreams,
Enduring through life's winding streams.

Though tides may shift and seasons change,
Our essence stays, it will not wane,
A warrior's call, so deeply sung,
Enduring spirit, ever young.

Invincible Flame

Through shadows deep, a fire glows,
A beacon where the darkness flows.
Whispers fade, and fears disband,
As courage takes its mighty stand.

Embers dance in vibrant hues,
Rays of hope where despair brews.
Within the heart, that flame ignites,
Guiding paths through endless nights.

Life's trials bend but never break,
The spirit forged that none can shake.
Amidst the doubt and through the pain,
The invincible flame will always reign.

Soul's Awakening

In quiet dawn, the soul does wake,
From dreams untold, the vision takes.
Whispers of the morning light,
Guide the heart from restless night.

Within the depths of silent grace,
Reflections of an inner space.
The journey starts with gentle strides,
Into the realm where truth resides.

Awaken now, to life anew,
Embrace the path of what is true.
With every step, with every breath,
The soul reborn, defying death.

Rise Above

From valleys low, the call ascends,
To heights unknown, where vision blends.
Through chasms dark and mountains high,
The spirit soars into the sky.

Challenges like winds may howl,
Yet inner strength they can't defoul.
With wings of will, and heart so brave,
Rise above what others crave.

Onward, onward, break the mold,
In fearless flight, let dreams unfold.
Rise above the earthly bounds,
Where endless hope and love surrounds.

Echo of Determination

Through trails worn and paths untried,
With steely gaze, and shoulders wide.
The echo of determination calls,
And shatters doubt within its walls.

Every step, a testament,
To hopes and dreams, so firmly bent.
Overcome the fiercest foe,
With grit and grace, the spirit's glow.

In every heart, that echo sings,
Proclaiming strength, and what it brings.
Determined soul, forever true,
To forge its destiny anew.

Whispering Stars

In the midnight's silent embrace,
Where dreams and shadows play,
Stars whisper secrets to the night,
Moments stolen from the day.

Through the veil of twilight's kiss,
A cosmic dance alight,
Whispers carried on moonbeams,
Echo in the quiet night.

Galaxies paint the sky serene,
In hues of silver bright,
Each whisper, a tale untold,
In the canvas of the night.

Ancient songs of time unfold,
In whispers soft and true,
Beneath the stars' gentle gaze,
The night is born anew.

In the realm of silent stars,
Where whispers softly blend,
A universe of stories,
In the night, they transcend.

Solitary Triumph

A lone path through forests deep,
Where shadows softly creep,
The heart beats strong and steady,
A promise it must keep.

Mountains rise to kiss the sky,
Rivers flowing by,
A solitary spirit's call,
An echo in reply.

Challenges on every side,
Battles fought within,
Yet through the struggle and the strife,
A triumph shall begin.

With each step, the journey draws,
A vision from afar,
In solitary triumph found,
Beneath the evening star.

Past the trials of the day,
And through the darkest night,
A single soul's resilient call,
Emerges in the light.

Inner Harmony

In the stillness of the mind,
Where chaos finds no place,
A harmony begins to bloom,
In gentle, quiet grace.

Through the tides of thoughtless noise,
And whispers of the past,
Inner peace is softly found,
A moment meant to last.

In the dance of soul and heart,
A symphony starts to play,
Each note a gentle reminder,
Of the harmony of the day.

Whispers of the inner self,
Guide through paths unknown,
In the chamber of the heart,
A seed of peace is sown.

Within the silent interlude,
A melody takes flight,
In the stillness of the soul,
Harmony finds its light.

Daring to Soar

Beneath the sky's unfathomed blue,
Dreams take to the air,
Wings of courage dare to spread,
For ventures bold and rare.

Through clouds of doubt and fear,
A spirit starts to climb,
In the heart beats the resolve,
To conquer space and time.

Winds of fate may try to sway,
But dreams cut through the gale,
With steadfast eyes upon the prize,
The daring never fail.

Each ascent a testament,
To courage held within,
In daring to soar high above,
New journeys shall begin.

Beyond the heights of yesterday,
And skies not yet explored,
Lies the realm of fearless hearts,
Forever daring to soar.

The Inner Flame

Deep within where whispers hide,
A flame of hope does gently bide,
Through darkest nights it softly glows,
Guiding hearts where courage flows.

In silent chambers, fears dissolve,
With each breath, new strength evolves,
No storm can quench this inner light,
It conquers shadows, fuels the fight.

In moments stark, when doubts appear,
This flame burns bright, dispels the fear,
A beacon for the weary soul,
It leads us on, it makes us whole.

Through trials faced and triumphs won,
The inner flame will never shun,
Every spark a tale untold,
In its warmth, our dreams unfold.

Boundless Essence

Beneath the sky, limitless and blue,
A boundless essence flows right through,
In every leaf, in every stream,
Whispering the eternal dream.

Life's pulsing rhythm, strong and free,
Found in the earth, sky, and sea,
In endless cycles, night to noon,
It sings a everlasting tune.

A symphony that knows no end,
In every bend, around each bend,
It carries us from dusk to dawn,
In its embrace, we're never gone.

Infinite, vast, without constraint,
An essence pure, devoid of taint,
It binds us all in unity,
A single truth, eternally.

The Warrior's Journey

Across the fields of battles past,
The warrior's journey, shadows cast,
With every step, a tale of might,
In dawn's first glow and twilight's light.

Armor worn and sword in hand,
Through trials faced, they make their stand,
With honor bright, and spirit true,
They carve a path through skies of blue.

Each scar a badge, each wound a tale,
The warrior's heart will never fail,
Through storm and fire, calm and rain,
They rise again, defy the pain.

In victory or in defeat,
The journey, fierce, remains complete,
For in the end, it's not the fame,
It's how they played this valiant game.

Strength in Shadows

In shadows deep where secrets lie,
True strength is born, it cannot die,
Invisible, yet ever there,
A silent force beyond compare.

With every trial faced in night,
Courage blooms without the light,
Unseen by eyes, yet known within,
This strength defies the darkest sin.

Beyond the veil of doubt and fear,
A power grows, pristine and clear,
It lifts the spirit, steels the mind,
In shadows, pure resolve we find.

When light returns and shadows fade,
The strength within shall never jade,
For in the depths, we've learned to see,
The force that sets our spirits free.

Resilient Heart

Beneath the weight, I find the strength,
Emerging from the darkest night.
In shadows deep, I journey forth,
A beacon shining ever bright.

The storms may rage, the winds may wail,
Yet still I stand, with courage bold.
For in my chest, a heart that beats,
With tales of valor, yet untold.

Enduring trials, I rise anew,
Each scar a testament of grace.
With every fall, I rise again,
Unyielding in this endless race.

Faith in Me

In whispered dreams, I find my call,
A voice within, so clear and free.
Through every doubt, I rise above,
With steadfast faith, I trust in me.

The path is long, the journey hard,
Yet in my heart, a burning fire.
For through the night, and darkest days,
I reach for heights, and climb yet higher.

Belief in self, a guiding star,
Through tempest fierce, and trials vast.
With every step, I find the way,
And in my faith, I stand steadfast.

Vision of Triumph

Upon the crest of dreams I soar,
A vision bright, a triumph fair.
With every stride, the future calls,
And in its light, I cast my stare.

Through valleys low, and mountains high,
With steadfast will, I journey on.
For in my eyes, a gleam of hope,
A vision bright, that greets the dawn.

No fear can hold, no doubt can chain,
When destiny's within my sight.
For in my soul, a burning flame,
Ignites the path, and gives me flight.

Voice from Within

A whisper soft, yet strong and sure,
Of inner strength, I can't ignore.
From deepest heart, the voice resounds,
And guides my steps on life's vast shore.

It calls in times of fear and doubt,
A beacon bright, a guiding light.
Through trials fierce, its wisdom shines,
And leads me through the darkest night.

With every word, I find my way,
A path that's true, a course that's clear.
For in that voice, I place my trust,
And cast away the chains of fear.

Unseen Bravery

In shadows cast, where few will tread,
Lies courage, born of silent dread.
A whisper caught, a quiet scream,
The warrior walks in unseen dream.

Not all who fight are loud and bold,
Some stories hush, yet still unfold.
Their strength unseen, but not less real,
In quiet hearts, brave souls reveal.

Daylight masks the hidden scars,
No medals shine, no march of stars.
Yet in the dark, their valor glows,
Unseen warriors, few will know.

In life's deep, uncharted air,
These silent soldiers do declare.
Their battles fought with inner might,
An unseen bravery, endless night.

Beneath the veil of mundane sight,
Their spirits rise to silent height.
Heroes all, who walk this way,
Unseen bravery, night and day.

Skyward Dreams

Beneath the endless sky, we dream,
Of heights unknown, of vast esteem.
The clouds their arms, wide open sweep,
Inviting minds to wake from sleep.

Horizons stretch, where dreams take flight,
A canvas broad, both day and night.
In azure fields our visions soar,
Beyond the realm of what we bore.

From star to star, we chart a course,
A cosmic journey, infinite source.
With every dawn, new hope redeems,
Our souls alight with skyward dreams.

In twilight beams and dawn's embrace,
We chase the light with tireless pace.
The heavens call, a siren's song,
To dream is where we all belong.

Though grounded firm by earthly ties,
Our spirits reach for boundless skies.
Skyward dreams, our hearts imbed,
A future bright, a path ahead.

Echoes of Confidence

In the silence lurks a voice,
A soft yet firm, affirming choice.
Echoes whisper through the air,
A resonance of souls that dare.

With every step, conviction grows,
A current strong, unseen but flows.
Belief in self, a steady ground,
In every heart, an echo's found.

The shadows fade, the doubt retreats,
Confidence in subtle beats.
An anthem rising, clear and proud,
A voice that speaks without a crowd.

Reflecting back from walls and stone,
An inner strength that's newly grown.
In echoes, find the truth we seek,
A confidence, no longer meek.

Through life's terrain, with footing sure,
We walk with echoes, bold and pure.
Each echo grows, a symphony,
Of self-assured serenity.

Indomitable Will

Unyielding force in heart and bone,
A spirit forged from fire and stone.
No storm or trial could break apart,
The steadfast core of a willful heart.

Mountains rise, yet we ascend,
Through tempest wild, our path extends.
Though winds may rage and torrents spill,
We march with indomitable will.

Against the odds, we stand unbowed,
A silent roar in every crowd.
Determined eyes, unwavering gaze,
To forge ahead through life's thick haze.

In every setback lies a spark,
A chance to rise from out the dark.
A flame that fuels our every thrill,
The constant drive of an iron will.

With every breath, we claim our space,
No fear can hold, no doubt erase.
Our journey marks the strength instilled,
By soul and mind, indomitable will.

Majestic Underdog

In shadows deep, it finds its spark,
A beacon bright within the dark.
Against the odds, it rises tall,
Majestic force, it conquers all.

With quiet strength, it moves the tide,
A humble heart with boundless pride.
Relentless in its quest to prove,
A silent fire, it learns to groove.

The world may scoff and turn away,
But steadfast underdog will stay.
Through trials tough and paths so steep,
Its spirit soars, it does not weep.

For in the whispers of defeat,
It hears the drum of hidden beat.
Majestic in its breakaway,
The underdog shall have its day.

With every step, it builds its worth,
A testament to quiet birth.
From depths unknown, it finds its song,
Majestic underdog, so strong.

Self-Worth Symphony

Within the heart, a song does lie,
A symphony that cannot die.
Through storms of doubt and hills of fear,
Its melody will persevere.

Each note a truth, so pure, so clear,
A testament to what is near.
The self that rises, unafraid,
In this grand symphony is laid.

A harmony of strength and grace,
Reflected in its steadfast pace.
No outer voice can steal its tune,
For it will sing beneath the moon.

In every beat, a truth unfolds,
Of self-worth that the spirit holds.
Unveiling rhythms deep inside,
A symphony where dreams reside.

So let the music never cease,
A song of self in perfect peace.
For in this symphony so bright,
The worth of self finds endless light.

The Power of One

In moments small, great change is born,
A whisper breaks the quiet morn.
The power of a single voice,
Can forge a path, can make a choice.

One step can start a journey long,
One word can lift a spirit strong.
A droplet in the vastest sea,
Can ripple through eternity.

With courage found in every heart,
The power of one can make a start.
In unity or standing lone,
Its force, a truth by essence shown.

A single light in darkest night,
Can pierce the shadows, bring to light.
A solitary act of care,
Can breathe anew the spark of dare.

So never doubt what one can do,
In every soul, this power's true.
The change begins with you, with me,
The power of one will set us free.

Unshakable Spirit

Through trials fierce and tempest's roar,
The spirit stands, it asks for more.
Unshakable, it holds its ground,
In quiet strength, it can be found.

With heart that's forged in fires bright,
It faces dawn, it conquers night.
No storm can break its steadfast will,
In every breath, it rises still.

Challenges may come and go,
But through it all, the spirit knows.
That in the core where courage lies,
Unshakable, it never dies.

Through every fall, it learns to rise,
With hope anew, it lights the skies.
An endless force of pure resolve,
In every trial, it evolves.

So when the world begins to shake,
The spirit strong will never break.
Unshakable, it writes its fate,
In every moment, stands elate.

The Soul's Awakening

In dawn's embrace, the light unfolds,
A whisper of the day concealed.
With every ray, a story told,
The soul's awakening revealed.

Through shadows cast, we find our peace,
A tranquil dance of morn's delight.
The world in slumber, fears release,
As dreams take flight in dawning light.

In fields of gold, a soft caress,
The gentle breezes kiss the land.
Unveil the heart, undo the stress,
In nature's grace, we understand.

With every bud and bloom anew,
The promise of a fresh born sky.
Our spirits rise, like morning dew,
In life's embrace, we soar and fly.

Beyond the horizon, hopes ignite,
A canvas of the soul untamed.
The break of day, our guiding light,
In every heartbeat's whisper named.

Unyielding Heartbeat

Within the storm, a steady pulse,
An echo through the times of strife.
A wind that brushes, spirits waltz,
The heartbeat of our inner life.

Against the tide, we hold our ground,
A rhythm fierce and unafraid.
The echoes of a love profound,
In every beat, our truth displayed.

Through trials faced and shadows cast,
Our tempo never skips a beat.
The ties that bind, unyielding, vast,
In life's embrace, our hearts compete.

Love's melody, a timeless song,
Resonating through the years.
With every note, we grow more strong,
Dispelling doubts, dispelling fears.

From birth to dusk, the cadence flows,
An anthem bold, unbroken chain.
The heartbeat of our journey shows,
In steadfast love, we rise again.

Resilient Soul

Through broken dreams and fractured skies,
A spirit rises, breaks the dark.
With weary hands and hopeful eyes,
The resilient soul ignites a spark.

In fields of grey, where sorrow dwells,
A seed of strength begins to grow.
Against the storm and tolling bells,
The resilient soul's courageous glow.

Amid the wreckage, still we find,
The will to stand and face the pain.
In every step, by love entwined,
The resilient soul will rise again.

From deepest wounds, the light emerges,
Healing whispers in the night.
With every fall, with every surge,
The resilient soul embraces flight.

Unyielding heart, undaunted gaze,
Through trials harsh, in endless flame.
In shadows cast, through darkest days,
The resilient soul remains the same.

Infinite Possibilities

Beneath the sky, where dreams alight,
A canvas of the stars unfolds.
In realms of infinite twilight,
Our possibilities, untold.

With every breath, a door appears,
A path yet tread, a chance anew.
Through whispered hopes and silent fears,
The infinite comes into view.

In every moment, time expands,
A tapestry of could-be's spun.
Within our grasp, the future stands,
Infinite, as the rising sun.

Through valleys deep and peaks untamed,
Our spirits venture, reach for more.
In boundless space, we are unchained,
Infinite dreams at every door.

Beyond the now, the worlds await,
With endless skies and seas to see.
In endless dreams, we carve our fate,
Infinite possibilities, we'll be.

Roots of Tenacity

In soils deep, where dreams take root,
Amid the dark, they find their fruit,
With patience, strength, they stretch and strive,
Through stone and storm, they stay alive.

Beneath the weight of time and toil,
They coil around the hardest soil,
Unyielding, steadfast, they ascend,
Till through the earth, their leaves extend.

In hidden depths where few will see,
Their silent struggle to be free,
Resilience finds its humble start,
In every stem, a beating heart.

No tempest strong enough to break,
The will that makes foundations quake,
From seeds that cracked in cold duress,
Grow forests tall in tenaciousness.

Through winters bleak and summers bright,
They hold their ground with all their might,
And whisper softly to the sky,
We rise together, you and I.

Infinite Bravery

In the vast expanse where shadows dwell,
Courage emerges, where few can tell,
Among the whispers of the night,
A heart ignites, with fearless light.

Strength in silence, bold and fierce,
To pierce through darkness, hearts adhere,
A journey long, with steps unsure,
Each stride, a testament impure.

Through stormy seas and wild terrains,
The spirit rises, breaks its chains,
Unfaltering in its resolve,
In fire and ice, it will evolve.

For bravery knows no bounds or end,
To every challenge, it will bend,
From deepest valleys to peaks untold,
The brave transform, the weak behold.

And when the dust of battle clears,
Triumph stands where fell the fears,
Infinite paths forged by the few,
Infinite bravery, ever true.

Essence of Fortitude

In the quiet stillness of the morn,
A strength is found, unformed, unborn,
It breathes beneath the surface calm,
A force that's waiting, like a balm.

Through trials long and battles hard,
It stands as sentinel and guard,
Unshaken by the winds of fate,
Endurance holds at every gate.

In moments when the soul feels weak,
When shadows loom and futures bleak,
The essence stirs, a fervent flame,
Fortitude whispers out its name.

Not easily seen, but deeply felt,
In every heart where courage dwelt,
It binds the broken, mends the frayed,
And lights the path that hope has laid.

At journey's end, with strength renewed,
The soul reflects its fortitude,
A testament to battles won,
In every heart, this strength begun.

Guiding Light

Through darkest nights, when all seems lost,
A beacon shines without exhaust,
It leads the way with gentle grace,
A guiding light in any place.

When shadows cloak the weary road,
Its glow disperses every load,
With steadfast glow, it draws us near,
Dispelling doubt, erasing fear.

In triumph's wake or sorrow's shade,
It casts its beam, never to fade,
A path illuminated clear,
Inviting hearts to persevere.

No tempest wild, nor raging sea,
Can dim the light that sets us free,
A north star constant in the night,
Ever present, shining bright.

So trust in lumens pure and true,
To guide your steps and see you through,
With every dawn, the morning's cue,
Light guides, yours to pursue.

Soul Unleashed

In the stillness of the night,
Where shadows dance and dreams take flight,
A soul breaks free from earthly bind,
Chasing stars, new worlds to find.

Beyond the reach of mortal hand,
Where time does bow to dreams so grand,
It soars above, in realms untamed,
A flame unquenched, forever named.

No chains can hold, nor fetters tie,
The spirit's call to endless sky,
With every beat, a song unveiled,
The soul unleashed, its path regaled.

In whispers soft, yet voices loud,
It finds its way, among the crowd,
A testament to strength untold,
In stories bold, its fate unfolds.

Embrace the night, the fervor feel,
For in its heart, the soul reveals,
Its boundless quest, its endless flight,
In stardust trails, it leaves its light.

Echoes of Confidence

In dawn's first light, courage wakes,
A heart that beats, a hand that takes,
With steps so firm and gaze so clear,
It faces day, devoid of fear.

Amid the murmur of the crowd,
A voice rings true, a promise loud,
To stand with pride, unwavering bold,
In confidence, its story told.

Each challenge met, each trial shown,
A testament to strength alone,
For in the echoes of belief,
The spirit finds its sweet relief.

Through storms that rage and winds that howl,
A steady soul, it stands afoul,
Its roots are deep, its branches high,
In confidence, it claims the sky.

So let your voice be ever strong,
In life's grand stage, where you belong,
For echoes of your confidence,
Will shape the world, in your presence.

Quiet Resolve

In moments hushed, where silence dwells,
A quiet strength forever wells,
With gentle grace and steadfast heart,
It shapes its course, stands firm apart.

No need for roar or blinding light,
For strength is found in calmest night,
In whispered dreams and silent vows,
In quiet resolve, the spirit bows.

Through trials fierce that test the soul,
It moves with purpose, steady goal,
With every step, in peace it strides,
In shadows dark, true strength resides.

Though storms may rage and tempests blow,
The quiet heart, it always knows,
That in resolve, true power lies,
In silence, might, its spirit flies.

So trust the path your heart does choose,
In quiet strength, you'll never lose,
For in resolve, both calm and deep,
Your spirit's light will always keep.

The Inner Voice

In corridors of mind's vast space,
A whisper calls, a silent grace,
Guiding steps with gentle tone,
The inner voice, we're not alone.

Amid the noise of daily grind,
A soothing balm, a light to find,
It nudges forth, with wisdom old,
In quiet moments, secrets told.

No need for shouts or grand display,
This voice within will lead the way,
With whispers soft, yet ever clear,
It shines the path through doubt and fear.

In choices made, in paths unknown,
It sings a song that's all our own,
A guiding star, a beacon bright,
The inner voice, our source of light.

So listen close and heed its call,
For in its truth, we stand tall,
In whispers soft, our strength we glean,
The inner voice, where dreams convene.

Stronger Every Day

With every dawn, I start anew,
A heart so light, the skies so blue.
The trials faced, now fade away,
I'm stronger, stronger every day.

In whispered winds, I find my voice,
A song of courage, my choice.
With every step, I pave the way,
I'm growing stronger every day.

Beneath the moon's soft, silver glow,
Through unknown paths, I bravely go.
Resilient as the ocean's sway,
I'm feeling stronger every day.

The stars they guide, the night awakes,
My spirit soars, no longer breaks.
In every struggle, I will stay,
Becoming stronger every day.

With hope aflame, I'll face the skies,
In every tear, a strength lies.
And through the night, and through the gray,
I'll always be, stronger every day.

Bold Horizons

Beyond the edge where light meets shade,
A world unknown, where dreams are made.
With open hearts and fearless gaze,
We chase the bold horizons blaze.

The winds they call, they sing our names,
Through fields of gold, where wild hearts tame.
In every dawn, a fresh new phase,
We seek the bold horizons' maze.

Mountains tall and rivers wide,
Together we, in stride we'll glide.
Through every night and sunlit haze,
We find the bold horizons' ways.

Our spirits high, our wings unfurled,
In unity, we face the world.
With every step, our fears erase,
We greet the bold horizons' grace.

With courage fierce and dreams in sight,
We journey forth, through dark and light.
In every breath, new dreams we chase,
To reach the bold horizons' place.

Inner Quest

Within the soul, a silent call,
A journey deep, where shadows fall.
Through tangled paths, where fears infest,
I seek the truth, an inner quest.

In quiet thoughts, the answers lie,
Beneath the doubts, where hopes defy.
Through every dream, my heart confessed,
I find myself on this inner quest.

The mirrors show the hidden scars,
A map of pain, beneath the stars.
Yet courage grows, and I'm impressed,
By the strength within this inner quest.

The fears once held, now drift away,
Replaced by light of dawning day.
My spirit fierce, by peace caressed,
Empowered by this inner quest.

Through valleys deep and mountains high,
In every tear, a new ally.
With every step, my soul possessed,
I journey on this inner quest.

Journey to Me

In quiet moments, stars align,
A path unfolds, uniquely mine.
Through valleys deep and skies so free,
I walk the unknown, journey to me.

The echoes of the past, they fade,
A newfound strength, in me displayed.
Through every storm and surging sea,
I find myself, journey to me.

With steadfast heart, and eyes so clear,
I face the doubts, embrace the fear.
In whispers soft, a wise decree,
Guides my steps, journey to me.

The sunlight warm upon my face,
In every step, a gentle grace.
Through forests dense and ancient tree,
I wander on, journey to me.

With every breath, I'm more aware,
Of who I am, how much I care.
I carve my path, my destiny,
On this profound journey to me.

Journey to Self

In the quiet of dawn's embrace,
we voyage through realms unseen.
Seeking echoes of forgotten truths,
where soul and spirit convene.

Beneath the stars' soft, silvery hymn,
we tread paths both ancient and new.
In the mirror of time's reflections,
we uncover fragments of the true.

Whispers of old winds guide us there,
through forests of fears confined.
The compass lies within our hearts,
in the landscapes of our minds.

Mountains rise with each stride,
valleys of doubt recede.
On this endless quest for essence,
our inner light is freed.

Morning breaks with renewed grace,
shadows of night dispersed.
In the clarity of awakening,
we find our place, traversed.

Relentless Spirit

In the fires where resolve is forged,
steps of valor make their way.
Unseen hands weave destiny's cord,
dreams ignite the break of day.

With wings of will, we soar above,
trials turn to distant lore.
Through the tempest, through the dark,
we find strength like never before.

Heartbeats echo in the night,
drumming to a relentless beat.
Within the chaos, sparks ignite,
turning challenge into feat.

Unyielding in the face of plight,
undaunted by the shadows cast.
The spirit shines with boundless light,
a testament to a journey vast.

Rising on the crest of hope,
the dawn unfurls its golden thread.
In its glow, we find our scope,
with courage born and spirit fed.

Majestic Core

In the cavern of life's great hall,
a majesty unseen resides.
Echoes of pure essence call,
in the heart where truth abides.

Rivers surge with ancient fire,
mountains crest in regal grace.
Nature's pulse beats ever higher,
in the core we each embrace.

Oceans whisper secrets grand,
forests hum with wisdom old.
In their rhythms, understand
tales of bravery, love bold.

From the depths to skies above,
the world within us swirls.
With each breath, we touch this love,
precious, vast as pearls.

Unity in paths we tread,
majestic core, our guide.
In its truth, we are led,
to where our dreams reside.

Radiant Essence

Through the veil of morning's light,
a glow of life begins to spread.
Radiant essence, pure and bright,
with a promise of days ahead.

In the dance of golden rays,
hopes and dreams take flight anew.
Shadows melt in warmth's embrace,
as past and present bid adieu.

Each beam a whisper in the air,
telling tales of endless skies.
Awakening hearts to care,
where eternal sunshine lies.

With every step, the light within,
grows stronger, fiercer, undiminished.
Guiding through the fleeting din,
until the night's edge is finished.

Radiance flows in heart's pure fire,
illuminating paths we trod.
In its glow, we all aspire,
reflecting the essence of a god.

Fearless Essence

In the depths of silent night,
Courage blooms, takes its flight,
Whispers turn to bold decree,
Fearless essence, wild and free.

Through shadows dark, paths untread,
Strength emerges, no words said,
Every step, a chosen quest,
In each heartbeat, we invest.

Mountains rise, vast and steep,
Yet our dreams, we shall keep,
With the dawn, we forge anew,
Fearless hearts, bold and true.

Beyond the veil, clear and bright,
Stars will guide our fearless plight,
Embrace the unknown, conquer the test,
In fearless essence, we find our best.

Silent echoes of the soul,
In unity, we find our role,
Boundless spirits, hearts' demand,
Fearless essence, hand in hand.

Divine Inner Voice

In the stillness of the mind,
Whispers soft and undefined,
Voices rise, sweet and clear,
Divine inner voice, ever near.

Guiding light through darkest days,
Silent truths in subtle ways,
In each breath, a sacred part,
Divine whispers in our heart.

Through the chaos, through the noise,
Find the peace in gentle poise,
Inner echo, pure and wise,
Divine revelation, hearts' rise.

In the quiet, answers found,
Love and grace abound, surround,
Listen deep, trust the sound,
Divine inner voice profound.

Every soul's a sacred tome,
Find the path to call it home,
Unveil the light, rejoice,
In the divine inner voice.

The Rising Phoenix

From the ashes, born anew,
Flames of gold, vibrant hue,
Rising high, a fiery arc,
Phoenix spirit, burning spark.

Through the trials, through the flame,
Every scar, a bold new name,
Rebirth's power, fierce and bright,
Phoenix soaring, endless flight.

Wings of fire, hearts ablaze,
Through the night into the rays,
Hope ignited, dreams ascend,
Phoenix rising, wounds to mend.

Every end, a new beginning,
Cycles turn, always spinning,
Rise again from shadows dark,
Phoenix legend, timeless mark.

Embrace the flame, let it grow,
Phoenix spirit, thrive and glow,
Born of fire, strong and free,
Rising phoenix, we shall be.

Visionary Heart

In the chambers of the soul,
Visionary heart takes control,
Dreams unfurl, wings of light,
Guiding through the endless night.

Eyes that see beyond the veil,
Spirit strong, will prevail,
Horizons wide, wisdom's part,
Guided by a visionary heart.

In the weave of time and space,
Blazing trails, we find our place,
Every dream, a work of art,
Crafted by a visionary heart.

Through the darkness, find the way,
In the light of breaking day,
Creation's pulse, a rhythmic start,
Driven by the visionary heart.

Boundless realms within our gaze,
Paths of stars, destiny's maze,
Trust the dream, let it impart,
Guide us, visionary heart.

Uncharted Brilliance

In lands where dreams gently flow,
Beyond the realms we dare to know,
A spark of brilliance, pure and bright,
Illuminates the endless night.

Mystic paths and stars align,
Guiding souls through space and time,
Unseen hands weave through our fate,
Opening doors we've yet to date.

Whispers of the brave unknown,
Echoes of adventures grown,
Each shadow hides a vibrant hue,
A canvas calling me and you.

Stars can fall, but still they rise,
In endless splendor, night's disguise,
In every failure, lessons bloom,
Within the vast, creative room.

So, chart your course through dark and calm,
With fearless heart and open palm,
For in the depths of mystery,
Lies brilliance, waiting to be free.

Glimmer of Assurance

In the storm's most frantic wail,
Hope's faint whisper tells a tale,
Of promises that light the path,
Guiding from despair and wrath.

A flicker in the darkest night,
Sings softly of the coming light,
Assurance, like the dawn's embrace,
Warms the cold and quiet space.

Through valleys shadowed, steep and deep,
Through battles where the strong may weep,
An inner calm, steadfast and true,
Glimmers with a golden hue.

Each step, though cautious, still is strong,
To face the fears we've held so long,
For in our hearts, we trust the spark,
That leads us through the deepest dark.

So hold the glimmer close and near,
It banishes the greatest fear,
In each unknown, and trails afar,
Assurance shines just like a star.

The Power Within

In each heartbeat, silent might,
Lies a force to conquer night,
Whispers of a fierce command,
Buried deep within our hand.

When shadows loom and doubt does call,
Stand tall and let your spirit stall,
For inner fires do brightly burn,
With lessons that we all must learn.

Against the tide, the strength we find,
In courage's grasp and steady mind,
No storm can take the will to fight,
When anchored in our inner light.

Through trials vast and oceans wide,
The power within serves as the guide,
It lifts the weary, heals the scar,
And carries dreams from near to far.

So harness what's within your soul,
For you are part of something whole,
An energy, pure and divine,
The power within makes you shine.

Inner Strength

In moments fragile, tender frail,
When might appears to surely fail,
Silent whispers, brave and strong,
Remind the heart where we belong.

Through tempests wild and winds that moan,
We find our courage, safe alone,
Unyielding force, untouched by plight,
A beacon in the darkest night.

Strength is found in quiet peace,
In letting past our fears release,
It's not the loudest voice that wins,
But steady hearts where strength begins.

In every tear, in silent cries,
Resilience forms, and never dies,
With every step, through pain and strife,
Inner strength preserves our life.

So heed the call within your soul,
For inner strength will make you whole,
In battles fought within the mind,
This silent strength you'll always find.

Whisper of Hope

In the quiet of the night,
A whisper soft as breeze,
Carries dreams of distant light,
To set our souls at ease.

In the garden of our dreams,
Where shadows cast away,
Hope's whisper softly streams,
Bringing dawn to break the gray.

Through the tempest, through the storm,
Its voice can still be heard,
Binding hearts in gentle form,
With every whispered word.

In the silence, in the dark,
Its melody will play,
A beacon, bright and stark,
Guiding hearts that stray.

Whispered softly, yet so clear,
A song that won't depart,
Hope remains forever near,
A whisper to the heart.

Shadows of Strength

In shadows deep and long,
Where sunlight fears to tread,
We find a strength, so strong,
To raise our weary head.

When trials come our way,
And darkness paints the sky,
It's then we hear the say,
Of strength that makes us fly.

Through forest dense and wild,
Where fears are bold and new,
Our strength, though meek and mild,
Sees every journey through.

No shadow can erase,
The light within our soul,
It's there we find the grace,
To stand and make us whole.

In every shadow cast,
A glimmer hidden deep,
Strength that holds us fast,
In shadows, let it seep.

Courageous Journey

Upon the path we tread,
With courage in our stride,
Each step we do not dread,
With hope and heart as guide.

Through valleys low and steep,
And mountains rising high,
Our hearts the courage keep,
To soar beyond the sky.

When winds of doubt do blow,
And fears begin to creep,
We let our courage show,
And leap into the deep.

A journey, long and vast,
With trials yet unknown,
Our courage binds us fast,
And marks the seeds we've sown.

Onward, ever onward,
To dreams we hold so tight,
Our journey, bold and onward,
With courage as our light.

Inner Harmony

Within the soul's deep sea,
Where waves of thought do roll,
Lies calm and harmony,
A peace to make us whole.

Each breath a gentle tide,
In rhythm, life does sing,
A melody inside,
To which our hearts do cling.

Amidst the chaos loud,
And clamor of the day,
A peace within the shroud,
Finds harmony its way.

In every silent beat,
A symphony untold,
Where inner worlds do meet,
And harmony takes hold.

From depths, a whisper pure,
A song of tranquil flow,
Inner harmony, sure,
In every heart does grow.

Rise and Shine

Awake the world with morning's gleam,
Embrace the day, fulfill your dream.
The sky alights with hues so bright,
Onward now, into the light.

Each dawn presents a brand-new start,
A chance to flourish, play your part.
With courage rise, your spirit free,
In every ray, your destiny.

Feel time's embrace in every hue,
A canvas vast, awaiting you.
The morning whispers, rise and shine,
This day is yours, it is divine.

Echoes of dawn within your soul,
Inspire the heart to meet its goal.
With every step, with every breath,
Emerge anew, outshine the rest.

Awake, arise, the world is wide,
A journey grand, your own to guide.
Embrace each sunray from above,
For in its light, you'll find your love.

Wings Unfolding

Within the heart, a whisper stirs,
A calling deep, the soul prefers.
To spread its wings, to feel the air,
A journey vast beyond compare.

Break forth the chains and rise above,
Embrace the sky, the flight of love.
With every beat, the wings unfold,
A story timeless, brave, and bold.

The horizons call, a siren's plea,
Boundless dreams across the sea.
From mountain peaks to valley low,
On wind and whisper, dare to go.

Each current lifts, each breeze inspires,
A dance of hope, with pure desires.
With wings unfurled, the world you greet,
The boundless sky beneath your feet.

So dare to dream, so dare to fly,
Let vision lead through open sky.
In every soar, in every dive,
Find freedom's call and truly thrive.

Path to Greatness

A journey long, with steps so true,
Each moment bright, with goals to pursue.
With every mile, with every trial,
Your spirit strong, your heart will smile.

Mountains high and valleys deep,
Promises within you keep.
With steady stride, you'll reach the crest,
For in your heart, you know you're blessed.

Belief alone will guide you far,
Through darkened night, to morning star.
With purpose clear, your path conferred,
A whispered dream becomes your word.

Challenges may block your way,
But courage strong will never sway.
With heart aglow and eyes aligned,
You'll find the strength within your mind.

So onward march, with head held high,
Beneath the boundless, open sky.
For greatness lies in how you strive,
In every step, in every drive.

Unyielding Soul

When shadows fall and night prevails,
An inner light still speaks its tales.
Through storms and trials, rough or mild,
The soul remains, forever wild.

With steadfast heart and courage true,
No obstacle can shadow you.
Boundless strength within you rise,
Like morning sun in endless skies.

Each setback forms a greater climb,
With every fall, an upward chime.
Through every tear, through every pain,
The spirit soars, it shall remain.

Unyielding soul with power immense,
In every trial, without pretense.
With fervent hope and dreams in sight,
It conquers fears, it trusts the light.

So forge ahead, let spirit lead,
In every want, in every need.
For in your core, a strength untold,
Unyielding soul, forever bold.

Embrace the Flame

In the heart of night we linger,
Shadows dance and secrets prowl,
Flicker softly, tender finger,
In the hush the fires growl.

Courage born from amber's light,
Blaze within, relentless call,
Ignite the hope, dispel the fright,
Rise again, defeat the fall.

Warmth of dreams enshrined in gold,
Ancient tales, the embers tell,
Whispers of the bold and old,
In the glow our spirits dwell.

Fuel the fire, night adjourns,
Phoenix spreads its wings on high,
Kindled heart in fervor burns,
Flames ascend to touch the sky.

Embrace the flame, fear not the heat,
Forge anew with passion bright,
In its glow our souls complete,
Dance within the fire's light.

Roots of Steel

In the soil, deep and hidden,
Strength and tenacity combine,
From the earth our dreams unbidden,
Stretch to realms divine.

Through the storm and winds unyielding,
Boughs may bend but roots remain,
From the core life's force is wielding,
Hope, enduring through the strain.

Mountains tremble, rivers veer,
Yet the heartland stands unmoved,
In the depths a power near,
Roots of steel, forever proved.

With each dawn our resolve grows,
Iron wills rise with the sun,
Steadfast through the ebb and flows,
Battles fought, and victories won.

Hold the ground, unwavering,
Roots of steel our foundations keep,
In the strength of earth's embracing,
Find the fortitude we seek.

Heart's Whisper

Beneath the stars, as night descends,
Silent echoes softly speak,
In the quiet, love extends,
Messages the heart may seek.

Gentle breezes through the leaves,
Carry secrets, truths unfold,
In the stillness, heart believes,
Whispers silver, pure, and bold.

Sentiments with threads enspun,
Woven through the realms of night,
Touch the soul, every one,
Guiding us with tender light.

Quiet murmurs, soft and clear,
Words unspoken, deeply true,
In the heart, they persevere,
Promises in skies of blue.

Listen close, these whispers heed,
Heart's soft voice, a guiding song,
In its rhythm, find the seed,
Love eternal, ever strong.

Awakening Strength

In slumber deep, the spirit wakes,
Stirs the dawn with gentle touch,
Silent strength within us quakes,
Whispers speak of power such.

Through the veil of night comes light,
Rays that break through shadows frail,
Signs of courage shining bright,
Inner fortitude prevails.

Every step, a bold embrace,
Challenges are met with grace,
Find the strength in softest place,
Within the heart, a sacred space.

Awakening with every breath,
Strength anew, our spirits rise,
Conquer fears, no bonds of death,
Lifted by the morning skies.

In the dawn, our strength revealed,
Newfound power, firm and true,
With each moment, heart unsealed,
Rise, embrace what we renew.

Champion of the Soul

In battles fierce, where shadows play,
The heart reveals its brave array.
With every step, a story told,
The soul remains steadfast and bold.

Through storms unceasing, thunder's roar,
The spirit finds its wings to soar.
Unyielding to the darkest night,
It rises, seeking out the light.

A champion forged in fire's embrace,
Defying odds, they find their place.
With courage drawn from depths unknown,
They conquer fears, they stand alone.

Resilient through the tests of time,
Their song becomes a timeless rhyme.
For in the heart where dreams reside,
The soul's true strength is magnified.

Each victory, a testament,
To battles fought, to time well spent.
A champion in heart and mind,
Through every trial, their path defined.

Brilliance Unfolded

A spark ignites the quiet air,
A beacon bright beyond compare.
In shadows where the doubts reside,
A brilliance seeks its place to bide.

From tendrils dark, a light is born,
Breaking dawn, a brand new morn.
A wisdom deep within unveiled,
Where once the heart and mind had failed.

Illuminating paths unseen,
Where dreams and reality convene.
The universe in silent praise,
Admires this incandescent blaze.

Emerging from the vast unknown,
A spirit in its glory grown.
With every breath, a life anew,
A world of endless hues in view.

Brilliance glows, it never fades,
In hearts where its light pervades.
A journey writ in golden script,
With every chapter, free and flipped.

The Mind's Fortress

Within the mind, a fortress stands,
A citadel of iron bands.
Guarding thoughts both wild and tame,
This bastion holds the world in frame.

Through turmoil vast and trials fierce,
No storm shall breach its steadfast tiers.
With gates of wisdom standing tall,
It weathers every rise and fall.

Foundations set in granite clear,
Reside the hopes, the dreams held dear.
Each wall adorned with visions bright,
A gale resisting, towering height.

Solitude and peace within,
A sanctuary from the din.
In quiet halls, the answers seek,
A mind's reprieve, the strong, the meek.

This fortress built with thoughts so grand,
Endures eternal, strong it stands.
For in the mind, where echoes play,
A silent strength shall lead the way.

Whispers of Potential

In every heart, a whisper dwells,
A tale of futures, bold it tells.
In hushed tones, where dreams ignite,
It flutters softly, taking flight.

Beneath the layers, deep inside,
Potential waits, a rising tide.
With every breath, it learns to grow,
A silent force, a steady flow.

In moments small, in acts of grace,
The whispers find their rightful place.
Unfolding futures yet untold,
In whispered breaths, a life of gold.

Encouraged by the light of day,
The potential wends its gentle way.
Bound not by fear, nor muffled fear,
But boundless hope that rings so clear.

In silence heard by listening hearts,
The whispers carve their sacred parts.
A symphony of dreams set free,
A chorus of what yet shall be.

Boundless Courage

In the heart of shadows deep,
Where whispers haunt and serpents creep,
A light unseen, yet fiercely bold,
Ignites the courage to unfold.

With steps unsure on paths unknown,
The seeds of fear are overthrown,
For in each breath, a strength anew,
Boundless courage to pursue.

The winds may howl, the storms may rage,
Yet bravely we turn each page,
In tales of old and mirrors bright,
We find our way, ignite the night.

When mountains loom and valleys yawn,
And hope seems barely hanging on,
A whisper soft, a shout of cheer,
Boundless courage drives out fear.

In every heart and every soul,
A spark persists, a burning goal,
To face the dark with steadfast grace,
Boundless courage, our saving embrace.

Daring to Dream

In the quiet of the night,
When stars whisper dreams so bright,
A soul unfurls its hidden wings,
Daring to dream of wondrous things.

Beneath the veil of mundane life,
Where worries cut like sharpened knife,
A hope takes root and starts to grow,
Daring to dream, to break the flow.

When doubts encircle like a chain,
And daylight brings its share of pain,
A vision clear begins to gleam,
Daring to dream, despite the seam.

With every step on untried ground,
Where fear and faith entwine and bound,
A heart beats strong, a light supreme,
Daring to chase the grandest dream.

In every life where shadows fall,
And silence answers every call,
There lies a spirit, calm yet keen,
Daring to love, to hope, to dream.

Self-Reliance

In the quiet still of dawn,
Where whispers of the night have gone,
A lone star glows in skies serene,
Self-reliance, soft yet keen.

When paths diverge in tangled wood,
And no one's there, but if you could,
Find strength to rise from deep inside,
Self-reliance will be your guide.

Though storms may break and winds may tear,
And fleeting comfort's never there,
A touch of faith, a gleam of pride,
Self-reliance walks beside.

In moments when the heart feels small,
And shadows stretch across the hall,
A spark ignites, begins to glide,
Self-reliance won't subside.

Through trials harsh and lessons tough,
When all seems lost or not enough,
A will, a fire, a soul undenied,
Self-reliance fortified.

The Warrior Inside

Amid the echo of the fray,
Where shadows dance and doubts replay,
A heart stands tall, a soul complete,
The warrior inside won't retreat.

Through every thorn and winding maze,
In darkest nights, through endless days,
A fire burns, a flame so wide,
The warrior lives, won't be denied.

When silence falls, a deadly hush,
And hope begins to feel the crush,
A strength unseen, a shield, a guide,
The warrior inside won't subside.

Through trials long and battles fierce,
Where every wound and cut, and pierce,
Each scar that heals with painful pride,
The warrior holds, deep inside.

In every soul there lies a fight,
A will to climb, to grasp the light,
With heart so fierce and eyes open wide,
The warrior inside, our eternal guide.

Fearless Pursuit

In the heart of night so deep,
Where shadows dance, and spirits leap,
A spark ignites, a dream takes flight,
Chasing stars, defying night.

Through tangled woods and stormy seas,
The path is rough, yet strides with ease,
With every step, courage grows,
In fearless pursuit, destiny glows.

Mountains tall, and valleys low,
Fear dissolves like melting snow,
Eyes fixed on the distant crest,
Unyielding spirit, never rest.

Amidst the thorns, a rose unfurls,
A beacon bright in a world of swirls,
Fearless hearts, forever true,
In every dawn, a dream anew.

To the edge of the earth's embrace,
With determined heart, and steadfast grace,
In the fearless pursuit of light,
We conquer the darkness of the night.

Limitless Horizons

Skies stretch wide, horizons clear,
Boundless dreams draw ever near,
Beyond the edge of what we see,
Lies the realm of possibility.

Wings of hope take flight in skies,
To realms where aspirations rise,
No borders hold, no chains confine,
In boundless hearts, the stars align.

Through fields of gold, and oceans blue,
Chasing visions pure and true,
The world is vast, yet hearts expand,
To limitless horizons, hand in hand.

In the whispers of the breeze,
Lie songs of distant galaxies,
With every breath, we come alive,
To explore, to dream, to strive.

Where land meets sky, and dreams unfold,
A tapestry of stories told,
In limitless horizons' sight,
We journey forth, into the light.

Embrace the Challenge

In every climb, a test of will,
Through valleys deep, and moments still,
Challenges rise, but so do we,
Embrace the struggle, set hearts free.

Against the tide, we forge ahead,
With every step, courage fed,
In trials faced, our strength is found,
Feet firm upon unsteady ground.

The mountain's peak, a daunting sight,
Yet in our hearts, a guiding light,
With gritted teeth, and spirits high,
We face the challenge, touch the sky.

In every fall, we rise anew,
With lessons learned, and clearer view,
Through storm and strife, we find our way,
In challenge found, a brighter day.

So bring the trials, bring the fight,
For in the end, we see the light,
Embrace the challenge, bold and true,
For in each battle, strength we accrue.

Sovereign Self

In the quiet of our minds,
A sovereign self, true heart finds,
No chains can hold, no ties constrain,
A spirit free from earthly pain.

Eyes that see beyond the veil,
Ears that hear life's gentle tale,
A soul that dances with the breeze,
In inner peace, we find our ease.

Through trials faced and battles won,
Through every dusk, and rising sun,
The sovereign self, with unshaken grace,
Leaves an indelible, lasting trace.

In the mirror's gaze, a calm reflects,
No fear, no doubt, no dark regrets,
A mind that's clear, a heart that's pure,
In sovereign self, we find our cure.

With every breath, a step in stride,
No limits bound, no doors are wide,
In sovereign self, we truly thrive,
In every moment, truly alive.

Path of Assurance

In twilight's tender hue,
A path paved clear and bright
Hope whispers to pursue,
Dreams beyond the night.

Each step a tale to tell,
Of courage deep and strong;
In life's vast carousel,
Where heart and soul belong.

Through shadows dark and wide,
The way stays firm and true;
With faith our constant guide,
New worlds we will imbue.

In stillness and in storm,
Assurance lights the way;
In every shape and form,
It leads to break of day.

So walk with trust in hand,
On paths of sure delight;
For in this steadfast land,
The future shines so bright.

Leap of Faith

A moment caught in time,
When doubt begins to break,
With courage so sublime,
A leap of faith we take.

Beyond what eyes can see,
Lies possibility;
In dreams where hearts fly free,
There lies our destiny.

One heartbeat to decide,
To jump and not to fall;
In trust's embrace we bide,
And answer to the call.

The unknown we behold,
With wings untied we soar;
In stories yet untold,
We find we're so much more.

So leap with heart so bold,
And cast away the fear;
For in that brave unfold,
A new world will premiere.

Embrace the Horizon

The dawn breaks tender light,
Upon a world so wide;
Inviting us to sight,
The dreams where we reside.

Horizons call us forth,
To places yet unseen;
With courage and with worth,
We walk where hearts convene.

In every breath we take,
A promise to explore;
In every move we make,
We open one more door.

Embrace the edge of now,
And let the future sing;
To past we need not bow,
In present, find your wing.

So journey without end,
Through skies both near and far;
Horizon as your friend,
No limit to your star.

Steadfast Will

In thickets dense and wild,
A force unyielding stands;
A will not mild nor child,
But strength in earnest hands.

Through tempests fierce and bold,
Its roots dig deep and wide;
Against the storm's harsh cold,
In fortitude, it'll bide.

A will as stone and steel,
Resilient through the fray;
No force can make it kneel,
Nor turn its gaze away.

When doubt and fear arise,
This will, they cannot shake;
With steadfast in its eyes,
A future bright to make.

So carry forth this might,
Through shadows dark and still;
For in the darkest night,
Prevails the steadfast will.

My Own Hero

In the quiet of the storm's embrace,
I find my strength, my saving grace.
The world may falter, shadows grow,
Within, a hero's heart does glow.

Undaunted by the darkest night,
It's in myself I see the light.
With every step on paths untold,
My courage fierce, my spirit bold.

The battles waged, both lost and won,
Through clouds, I chase the rising sun.
In mirrors, I see not just me,
But a warrior yearning to be free.

For in the depths of fear and doubt,
It's there my hero's self cries out.
No need for capes or songs of praise,
I rise, resilient, through the blaze.

Dreams Unbridled

In the vast expanse of endless skies,
My dreams take wing, to soar and rise.
Unshackled hearts, with visions clear,
They dance with stars, no trace of fear.

Through meadows lush with morning dew,
They chase horizons, ever new.
No mountain tall, no river wide,
Can stem the flow, can break their stride.

With each dawn's kiss upon the earth,
They find anew their place of birth.
Boundless, free, in cosmic flight,
They revel in the pure delight.

So let them roam, these dreams unbound,
In whispers soft or joyful sound.
For in their journey, vast and wide,
All hopes and wishes safe reside.

Inner Fire

In the quiet, deep within,
Lies a fire, bright, akin.
To the sun, in twilight's glow,
Its embers burn, though winds may blow.

Born of passion, fierce and true,
Its light a path, forever new.
Through trials faced, and sorrows worn,
This inner fire does not mourn.

Even in the coldest night,
It stands steadfast, burning bright.
A beacon in the darkest hour,
A testament to endless power.

So feed this flame, your inner core,
Let it blaze, forever more.
For within its warmth, its glowing pyre,
Lies the truth of your desire.

Silent Determination

In silence, strength is often found,
A quiet force, a steadfast ground.
No need for shouts, or grand displays,
Just steady steps through winding ways.

When faced with walls that tower high,
It's in the calm we learn to fly.
For silent hearts can hold great might,
With every beat, they rise in flight.

Determined paths, though oft unseen,
Are carved by those who live the dream.
In shadows deep, they find the way,
To turn the night into the day.

So trust in silence, in its song,
For in its depths, you will belong.
Silent strength, a fierce creation,
The root of true determination.

Stride of Assurance

Walk with purpose, eyes agleam,
In fields of doubt, let courage stream.
Through shadows deep, where fears cascade,
Steadfast steps, none can dissuade.

A heart ablaze with inner light,
Guides the soul through darkest night.
Whispers of strength, the spirit chants,
With every stride, the self enchants.

Mountains tall and valleys low,
Feet refuse to falter, slow.
In every beat, assurance rings,
Boundless hope on tireless wings.

A journey carved by hand and heart,
With love and faith, it won't depart.
Stride on bold, and never fear,
The path to dreams is ever clear.

Each step taken, none in vain,
Through joy and through the deepest pain.
Stride of assurance, brave and true,
The world unfolds its gifts to you.

Seeker of Dreams

Eyes that wander, soul that seeks,
Through the nights and through the weeks.
Dreams unfurl like morning mist,
Chasing whispers on the breeze's twist.

Stars align in cosmic dance,
Guiding on with silent glance.
In the hearts of seekers bright,
Burns a flame through the infinite night.

Footsteps left on sands of time,
Each a note in a mystic chime.
With every turn and winding bend,
Dreams and fate begin to blend.

Cages break, the spirit flies,
In the endless, open skies.
Seeker of the unseen dream,
Beyond the known, into the gleam.

A quest of heart and boundless mind,
In the pursuit, true joy they find.
Seeker, on your path so rare,
Live your dreams, breathe the air.

Pioneering Spirit

Through the forests dense and wild,
Walks a pioneer, free and unbeguiled.
Charting paths no eye has seen,
In a world so vast, serene.

With compass heart and purpose clear,
Ventures forth without a fear.
Blazing trails where none have tread,
Pioneering dreams, gently spread.

Mountains high and rivers broad,
Never halt this fearless prod.
For in the spirit lies the spark,
To light the way, dispel the dark.

Crafting futures out of clay,
Turning night to brightest day.
Each endeavor, bold and new,
With a heart that sees it through.

Pioneering spirit, wild and true,
Dreams take flight, the world renew.
With every step, the unknown greets,
In the vastness, the soul completes.

Roots of Courage

Deep within the soil of time,
Lies a strength, profound, sublime.
Roots of courage, anchored deep,
In the heart where valor sleeps.

Through the storms of life's embrace,
Steady roots hold their place.
Branching out in growth and might,
Facing dawn and darkest night.

In the trials, courage grows,
With each challenge, spirit knows.
From the roots, the soul ascends,
In its journey, strength transcends.

Through the winds of change and fear,
Roots of courage, strong and clear.
In the earth and in the heart,
Firmly planted, plays its part.

Strength from roots, from depths unseen,
In the heart, where thoughts convene.
Roots of courage, silent guide,
Through this life, shall we abide.

Relentless Pursuit

Through stormy nights and weary days,
Determined steps mark out the way.
Undaunted by the looming haze,
A spirit fierce, come what may.

With dreams alight, the fire burns,
Each moment passes, it returns.
The mountains climb, the rivers churn,
The heart, relentless, ever yearns.

Eyes fixed ahead, the road unfolds,
With every challenge, courage holds.
A journey long, an epic told,
By one whose soul cannot grow old.

Beneath the weight of thousand fears,
A will unbroken, sage appears.
In pursuit of dreams through the years,
Triumph smiles through silent tears.

So onward through the realm of night,
The quest, a gleaming beacon's light.
Relentless, ever, in its flight,
The journey molds to endless might.

Journey of Heart

Through valleys low and peaks so high,
A heart's adventure under sky.
With beating wings, the soul shall fly,
In search of dreams that never die.

The love it seeks, through dusk and dawn,
A golden thread, so finely drawn.
Through winter's chill and summer's lawn,
A heart's desire, never gone.

The path is wrought with joy and woe,
Yet undeterred, it knows to go.
For in this journey, it shall grow,
And in its trials, strength will show.

In whispers soft, the winds relay,
The stories old, of time's ballet.
A heart that beats, as night meets day,
It's bound to find its cherished way.

So onwards in this life's parade,
With love's embrace, the path is laid.
The journey of the heart will shade,
A tapestry of dreams arrayed.

Stepping Stones

With cautious feet, we tread the ground,
Stepping stones in life abound.
Each step, a lesson to astound,
In silence, echoing profound.

On rugged trails, where hopes are sown,
Through joy and sorrow, we have grown.
The stones beneath through time are shown,
To guide us to the truth unknown.

In every leap, and every fall,
The stepping stones, they heed our call.
They build a bridge, both strong and tall,
To cross the futures that enthrall.

With hearts in hand and minds aware,
We navigate with tender care.
Each stone we step, a life to share,
In twilight's gleam or morning's flare.

So down this path, we walk with grace,
Our stepping stones in time and space.
They lead us to a cherished place,
A journey etched in life's embrace.

Inner Victory

Within the quiet of the mind,
A battle fought, where none may find.
With strength of heart, the threads unwind,
To claim a victory, undefined.

In shadows deep, where fears reside,
A spark of light begins to guide.
With whispered courage by your side,
The inner storm shall soon subside.

Through trials dark and struggles stark,
The soul ignites its radiant spark.
Surmounting every daunting arc,
It leaves behind an ancient mark.

Amidst the silence, voices clear,
An anthem rises, crystal, pure.
The triumphs echo, sincere,
A testament that shall endure.

In moments calm, reflect, and see,
The path to true serenity.
An inner victory, bold and free,
Embrace the strength inside of thee.

The Inner Beacon

In the quiet moments still,
A light emerges, strong at will,
Guiding through the darkest night,
A beacon burns, forever bright.

When shadows close the day away,
And hope seems lost in shades of gray,
The inner spark, it softly glows,
Reviving dreams as morning grows.

Within the heart, a flame is born,
Undeterred by storm or scorn,
A luminous path it carves in deep,
Promises made, it vows to keep.

Through valleys low and mountains tall,
Its guiding wisdom answers all,
In every soul, it whispers clear,
Hold steadfast, let go of fear.

As journeys end and new ones start,
This light remains within the heart,
A silent guide, our faithful star,
For every step, no matter how far.

Bravery Unbound

Beneath the veil of timid guise,
A valor waits with no disguise,
In whispered dreams of courage bold,
A heart of steel begins to mold.

When trials loom and fears arise,
Unyielding strength unveils its eyes,
Through every test and daunting plight,
Bravery shines its fiercest light.

No chains can bind this fearless force,
Nor turn its journey from the course,
With every stride, it paves the way,
For dawn to break the longest day.

In quiet acts or grand display,
It challenges the fierce dismay,
And in its wake, the shadows pale,
For bravery shall always prevail.

From deepest wells of hidden might,
It surfaces in purest light,
Unbound by doubt, it soars above,
A testament to boundless love.

Champion Within

In silence, where no eyes can see,
A champion sleeps in you and me,
Awaiting moments fierce and grand,
To rise and make a rightful stand.

With every heartbeat, strength is found,
Encouragements in whispers' sound,
No need for medals, praise, or fame,
A champion lives in every name.

Through victories small and battles won,
The inner flame shines like the sun,
Unyielding trust in self and kin,
The journey starts from deep within.

Beyond the doubts and past the fear,
A clearer voice begins to cheer,
With faith as fuel and heart as guide,
A champion, strong, will not subside.

In every soul, a war is fought,
Ambitions, dreams, and paths are sought,
Embrace the power, feel it spin,
And find the champion within.

Heart's Compass

In the quest for life's true north,
The heart's compass leads us forth,
Guiding with a gentle nudge,
Through moments grand and times we trudge.

Silently, with grace it points,
To paths unseen, to healing joints,
A navigator through the haze,
A constant light in doubtful days.

When choices cloud and roads divide,
It whispers truths we hold inside,
In every beat, a sage's clue,
To navigate the old, the new.

Compass of the soul's desire,
Stoking dreams with inner fire,
With trust in heart's unspoken word,
Our steps are sure, our journey stirred.

In times of calm or tempests wild,
It stays our course, both meek and mild,
Heart's compass, true and unrelenting,
Our lifelong path, always presenting.

Grace Under Pressure

In trials' embrace, we find our might,
When shadows grow, and day meets night,
Through tempest's roar, hearts take flight,
Grace under pressure, pure and bright.

As mountains quake with intense strain,
And storms unleash their wildest reign,
We stand unwavering, free of chain,
Embracing struggle without disdain.

Amid the chaos, spirits rise,
With strength untold, beyond the skies,
In darkest depths, our hope complies,
Grace under pressure, never lies.

Against the odds, we carve our way,
With inner light as our array,
Through every storm, come what may,
We find our grace, come break of day.

Resilient hearts, in trials gleam,
In toughest times, our souls redeem,
Grace under pressure, like a dream,
Guides us through, serene, supreme.

Emblem of Hope

In fields of gold, where dreams unfold,
An emblem shines, both brave and bold,
Through darkest nights, it keeps us told,
That hope remains, a hand to hold.

In every heart, a beacon warm,
Through life's wild dance, through every storm,
This symbol bright, of steadfast form,
Hope guides the soul, and keeps it warm.

When shadows cast their weary spell,
And fears arise, their tales to tell,
The emblem's light begins to swell,
Dispelling doubts, where worries dwell.

Through trials fierce, through unknown lands,
It graces paths, with gentle hands,
In faith and love, where each soul stands,
The emblem of hope, forever bands.

So hold it close, through every phase,
Its glow will shine, in darkest haze,
With hope in heart, the future's gaze,
Emblem of hope, in endless ways.

Unfolding Grace

As petals bloom in morning's light,
Unfolding grace takes gentle flight,
With every dawn, new hopes ignite,
A dance of life, both pure and bright.

In moments still, when time suspends,
Where silence speaks, and sorrow mends,
Unfolding grace, through life extends,
A touch of peace, the heart defends.

With whispered winds and tender streams,
In quiet nights, and moonlit dreams,
Grace finds its way, through endless seams,
Unfolding love, in radiant beams.

Through every storm, and trial's test,
It wraps us close, with gentle zest,
Unfolding grace, in hearts expressed,
A solace found, in shadows' nest.

So let it flow, in every breath,
With each new step, and even death,
Unfolding grace, beyond life's breadth,
A boundless gift, in love's bequeath.

Shield of Serenity

Through chaos wild, and endless strife,
A shield of calm, protects our life,
Serenity, like a soothing fife,
Guides us through, amid the rife.

When tempests roar, and shadows creep,
In tranquil arms, our fears we keep,
This shield of peace, so strong and deep,
Serenity's vow, in silence sweep.

Through winter's chill and summer's blaze,
In every dawn, its light portrays,
A steady calm, through darkened maze,
Shield of serenity, gently sways.

In moments harsh, when spirits break,
It gathers strength, for our own sake,
Serenity's shield, no world can shake,
A bastion firm, through trials great.

Forever close, in hearts it lies,
With soothing touch, it never dies,
Shield of serenity, through all sighs,
A timeless guard, under stretching skies.

Wings of Determination

Through stormy skies and darkest night,
Our dreams take flight on wings so bright.
With courage fueled by heart and might,
We soar above to endless height.

Challenges may bar our way,
But faith will guide us, come what may.
Persistence leads to brighter days,
In shadows turned by morning rays.

Though winds may try to steal our claim,
Resilient spirits fan the flame.
Unyielding strength will earn its name,
And lift us from the depths of shame.

With eyes on stars, we won't adhere
To doubts that whisper in our ear.
For in our hearts, the path is clear:
To rise, to shine, to persevere.

Faith in Your Own Path

The road you walk is ever true,
Paved by steps that are just for you.
With every choice and forward view,
You carve a journey, bold and new.

Let others speak their words of doubt,
Your heart's compass will find the route.
In quiet strength, don't dwell about,
For inner faith will guide you out.

In every twist and turning lane,
Where joys are found and learned through pain,
You'll find that loss is not in vain,
Each lesson's seed in you will gain.

Believe in dreams, no matter how
They're cast aside by others now.
Your spirit will not break nor bow,
On paths that fate and you allow.

The Heart Knows Best

In moments still when silence holds,
The heart, it whispers truths untold.
Through trials met and times of cold,
It's there our deeper selves unfold.

Listen close to beats within,
They tell of where your dreams begin.
A compass through the thick and thin,
The heart, it guides, through loss and win.

No echo from outside resounds
As clear as love that knows no bounds.
For in the heart, pure truth abounds,
In whispered rhythms, sacred sounds.

Trust in what the heart conveys,
Through winding paths and shadowed ways.
It lights the dark with gentle rays,
And leads you to your brightest days.

Hidden Hero

In shadows cast by life's bright stage,
Unseen, you turn another page.
With silent strength and quiet rage,
You write your tale, not bound by age.

The world may miss the deeds you do,
In whispers where the brave and true
Perform with grace, though out of view,
The light within outshines the blue.

For heroism's not a show,
It's in the acts where kindness grows.
In silent ways, through highs and lows,
It's there your inner power flows.

Though accolades may never find
The path you've walked, with heart inclined,
Your legacy is love refined,
A hero's soul, with peace enshrined.

Inner Strength Unveiled

In shadows deep, where fears reside,
A spark of light begins to guide.
The heart finds hope, it beats anew,
With courage strong, it sees it through.

Mountains high, yet souls ascend,
On winding paths that never end.
Though winds may howl and skies grow dark,
Inner strength ignites the spark.

When doubt invades, and tears may flow,
A silent force begins to grow.
From depths unseen, it rises tall,
A whispered power that conquers all.

Embrace the trials, face the night,
For dawn will come, bringing light.
In every challenge, find your key,
Unlock the strength that sets you free.

With every step, with every fall,
The spirit stands, defying all.
In quiet moments, hear the roar,
Inner strength revealed, forever more.

The Courage Within

In silent halls, where whispers fade,
A seed of courage, gently laid.
It takes root deep, within the soul,
And makes the weary spirit whole.

Through darkest nights and endless days,
A heart of steel finds unseen ways.
Behind each fear, the truth is clear,
Courage lives, it's always near.

When faced with trials, don't retreat,
Stand firm, and make your heart's beat.
For courage blooms in hardest times,
Its strength is woven in life's rhymes.

With every step into the unknown,
True grit and bravery are shown.
In every breath, despite the din,
We find the courage deep within.

Though paths be rough, and storms be wild,
Stand strong, unyielding, reconciled.
For in the heart, where hope begins,
We'll find the courage that always wins.

Rise of the Silent Warrior

Amid the chaos, hear the calm,
A warrior's heart, a healing balm.
In silence, power softly grows,
With each challenge, strength bestows.

No battles fought with sword in hand,
But inner wars, where spirits stand.
In quietude, resolve is found,
Silent warriors, honor-bound.

With every shadow, they arise,
Determined hearts, unwavering eyes.
In whispers loud, their call is heard,
A steadfast force in each word.

They face the world with gentle grace,
And wear resilience on their face.
Through every storm, through every tear,
Silent warriors persevere.

Their rise is quiet, yet profound,
In every breath, their strength is crowned.
From depths of silence, fierce and free,
The silent warrior's legacy.

Embrace Your Magic

In every heart, a magic lies,
A spark unseen, beneath the skies.
With every dream, with every breath,
This magic conquers life and death.

No need for wands, or spells, or charms,
The magic lives within our palms.
With open hearts, and minds that dare,
Embrace the magic, always there.

In moments small, in grand design,
This inner magic weaves its sign.
From whispered thoughts to roaring deeds,
It's magic that the spirit feeds.

To doubtless eyes, it may seem thin,
But older hearts, they see within.
The magic that exists in all,
Will rise anew, and never fall.

So hold it close, this truth inside,
With magic as your steadfast guide.
Embrace the magic, know its worth,
And spread its light across the earth.